Did you Know About the Apple Car??

A $10 Billion Failure

How an Iconic Tech Giant Stalled in the Race to Autonomy

Joe E. Grayson

Copyright © 2024 Joe E. Grayson, All rights reserved.

No part of this publication may be reproduced, distributed, or transmitted in any form or by any means, including photocopying, recording, or other electronic or mechanical methods, without the prior written permission of the publisher, except in the case of brief quotations embodied in critical reviews and certain other noncommercial uses permitted by copyright law.

Table of Contents

Table of Contents

Introduction

Chapter 1: The Birth of an Idea

Chapter 2: Project Titan Takes Shape

Chapter 3: The Why Behind the Wheels

Chapter 4: Hitting Speed Bumps

Chapter 5: Challenges of Innovation

Chapter 6: Apple's Expensive Gamble

Chapter 7: The Decision to Pull the Plug

Chapter 8: What Comes Next?

Conclusion

Introduction

In 2015, a sense of anticipation filled the air as Jony Ive, the visionary designer behind Apple's most iconic products, unveiled a concept unlike anything the company had ever attempted. It wasn't another sleek gadget or a revolutionary software update. Instead, Tim Cook, Apple's CEO, found himself seated inside a prototype of a minivan. This was no ordinary vehicle. The interior boasted luxurious wood and leather finishes, and there was one glaring omission: no steering wheel. The car was fully autonomous. A human voice actress posed as Siri, responding to commands to simulate what the future of driving might look like. The demonstration felt more like a mix of innovation and improv theater than a polished presentation. Yet, this moment marked the beginning of one of the most ambitious projects Apple had ever undertaken.

This book delves into Apple's bold journey into the automotive industry—a venture that promised to redefine mobility but ended in an extraordinary and costly failure. With nearly $10 billion spent over the course of a decade, the Apple Car project was a gamble that tested the limits of innovation, leadership, and ambition. By examining the motivations behind this endeavor, the technological and market challenges it faced, and the reasons it ultimately faltered, this story provides a rare glimpse into the complexities of pushing boundaries in one of the world's most competitive industries.

Through the chapters ahead, we will explore the initial spark of the idea, the relentless pursuit of technological breakthroughs, and the turbulent internal dynamics that derailed the project. We'll uncover the broader implications of Apple's venture and the lessons it offers to innovators and businesses navigating uncharted territories. This is a story of ambition, ingenuity, and the challenges of taking risks in the relentless pursuit of innovation.

Chapter 1: The Birth of an Idea

Apple's rise to prominence as a global technology powerhouse was built on a foundation of groundbreaking innovation and relentless ambition. From the sleek simplicity of the iPod to the transformative capabilities of the iPhone, the company consistently redefined the boundaries of what technology could achieve. By the late 2000s, Apple was not just a tech company; it was a cultural phenomenon, shaping the way people communicated, worked, and experienced entertainment. Under the visionary leadership of Steve Jobs, Apple thrived on its ability to take complex technologies and distill them into elegant, user-friendly products that resonated with consumers worldwide.

Amid this era of unparalleled success, Steve Jobs and Tony Fadell, one of the key architects of the iPod, entertained an intriguing idea during their walks in 2008: What if Apple ventured beyond personal devices and into the world of automobiles? Their discussions were far from casual musings. They delved into detailed questions about what an Apple-designed car might look like. How would the dashboard function? What materials would they use for the seats? How would the car be powered? Jobs, known for his ability to envision the future, considered these possibilities with serious curiosity.

Fadell later recounted that these conversations revealed a clear overlap between the components of a car and the elements of Apple's products: batteries, computing power, mechanical systems, and seamless integration.

Jobs acknowledged the potential, yet he was also pragmatic. He recognized the immense challenge of entering an industry so vastly different from the one Apple dominated. As Fadell recalled, Jobs often concluded their talks with a mix of excitement and realism, noting how constrained Apple already was with its existing projects. While the idea of building a car lingered in Apple's collective imagination, it was set aside—at least for the time being. These early conversations, however, planted the seeds for what would later become one of the company's most ambitious undertakings.

By the early 2010s, Tesla was beginning to redefine the automotive industry, proving that electric vehicles could be both practical and desirable. With the release of the Tesla Model S in 2012, the company demonstrated that EVs could achieve remarkable range, cutting-edge technology, and luxury appeal. This breakthrough wasn't just a win for Tesla; it was a pivotal moment for the broader automotive market, showcasing the potential to disrupt a century-old industry dominated by internal combustion engines.

Apple, a company that thrived on challenging the status quo, could not ignore Tesla's growing success. Tesla wasn't merely making electric cars—it was creating a lifestyle, much like Apple had done with its ecosystem of devices. The Model S's sophisticated touchscreen interface, over-the-air software updates, and seamless integration of technology echoed Apple's philosophy of combining hardware, software, and design into a unified product. The parallels were hard to miss.

For Apple, the automotive industry began to look like an untapped frontier for innovation. The idea of creating a car that embodied Apple's trademark design ethos and technological integration became increasingly compelling. Tesla had proven there was a market for electric vehicles, and Apple's leadership saw an opportunity to enter the space, leveraging their expertise in batteries, software, and consumer-focused design. If Tesla could disrupt an industry as entrenched as automotive manufacturing, why couldn't Apple?

This growing interest wasn't just driven by competition—it was also inspired by Tesla's ability to position itself as a leader in sustainability and innovation. Apple, already committed to reducing its environmental impact, saw the EV market as a way to align its values with a potential new product line. Tesla's rise underscored the opportunity for newcomers to make their mark in the automotive world, and for Apple, the stage was set to take its first steps toward creating a car of its own.

Chapter 2: Project Titan Takes Shape

In 2015, Apple made its ambitions in the automotive industry official—at least behind closed doors. Under the code name "Project Titan," the company began assembling a formidable team of engineers, designers, and industry experts to turn the vision of an Apple car into reality. At the helm was Steve Zadesky, a former Ford engineer and a seasoned Apple executive known for his contributions to the development of the iPod and iPhone. Zadesky's appointment signaled Apple's commitment to bringing the same level of innovation and design excellence to the automotive space that it had achieved in consumer electronics.

Over the course of that year, Apple rapidly expanded its ranks, bringing in talent from across the tech and automotive industries. The team eventually grew to approximately 1,000 members, a mix of seasoned automotive engineers and fresh minds eager to push boundaries. Apple also established a top-secret lab in Silicon Valley, where the team could experiment with cutting-edge technologies, from battery innovations to autonomous systems.

The sheer scale of this effort underscored Apple's seriousness. Unlike many of its previous ventures, this was not about refining existing markets but about entering entirely new territory. Reports suggested that the team's initial goals were nothing short of revolutionary: a fully autonomous electric vehicle with a design so distinct it would stand out in an already competitive market.

Zadesky's leadership provided the foundation for what could have been a landmark achievement. However, the scope of the project presented challenges from the outset. The team faced immense pressure to deliver not just a car, but an Apple car—something that would redefine transportation in the same way the iPhone had reshaped communication. This ambitious beginning marked the start of a journey that would take unexpected turns, revealing just how difficult it is to merge cutting-edge technology with the complexities of the automotive world.

Apple's ambitions for its car project were nothing short of groundbreaking. From the outset, the vision was to create a fully autonomous vehicle—a car that would require no driver, no steering wheel, and no pedals. This wasn't just a car; it was imagined as a redefinition of transportation itself. Passengers would sit facing each other in a sleek, minimalist interior that featured luxurious finishes, including wood and leather, and a central table that evoked the atmosphere of a futuristic lounge. The concept aimed to transform cars from mere vehicles into spaces for productivity, relaxation, or entertainment, seamlessly integrated with Apple's ecosystem of services.

This bold vision set Apple apart from traditional automakers and even from tech-forward competitors like Tesla. While others focused on incremental advancements in autonomous features, Apple planned to leapfrog those efforts and deliver a product that would render traditional driving obsolete. At the core of this ambition was Apple's desire to merge hardware, software, and services into a cohesive and transformative experience—precisely the kind of integration that had defined its success in consumer electronics.

As whispers of this audacious project began to circulate, hints of Apple's secretive efforts emerged in public. In 2015, reports surfaced of self-driving Dodge Caravans navigating the streets of San Francisco. Observers noted the presence of advanced sensor arrays on these vehicles, including cameras and LiDAR systems, sparking curiosity about their purpose. Investigative reporting quickly connected these sightings to Apple, with the vehicles reportedly leased under shell companies linked to the tech giant.

These public glimpses confirmed that Apple wasn't just exploring concepts in a lab—it was actively testing its autonomous driving technology on real roads. The sightings fueled speculation and excitement, with many believing Apple was on the verge of unveiling a revolutionary product. These early moves showcased Apple's commitment to pushing boundaries, but they also marked the beginning of a journey fraught with challenges, as the gap between ambition and reality would soon become apparent.

Chapter 3: The Why Behind the Wheels

Apple's foray into the automotive industry was driven by a blend of strategic vision and the allure of untapped potential. At its core, the company saw the car as the next great frontier for integrating hardware and software—a space where it could replicate its winning formula of seamless user experiences. With vehicles becoming increasingly dependent on technology for navigation, entertainment, and connectivity, Apple recognized an opportunity to bring its ecosystem into the heart of everyday transportation.

The integration of hardware and software had always been Apple's hallmark, and the car presented an ideal platform to elevate this to unprecedented levels. Apple's expertise in designing efficient batteries, intuitive interfaces, and powerful processors positioned it uniquely to create a vehicle that could outshine the competition. Imagine a car where everything, from navigation to climate control, was controlled through a unified Apple system, tailored to the user and synced with other Apple devices. This level of integration promised not just convenience but an entirely new way to think about mobility.

Beyond technology, Apple saw financial opportunities in this venture. With the automotive industry representing trillions of dollars globally, even a small slice of the market could significantly boost the company's revenue. Moreover, autonomous systems offered the potential for recurring income through subscriptions to Apple's services. From in-car entertainment to app usage during commutes, an Apple car could become a moving hub for the company's ecosystem, driving revenue in ways traditional automakers could not.

The appeal of autonomous systems added another layer of ambition. Self-driving technology wasn't just a novelty—it was a paradigm shift with the potential to transform how people live and work. Autonomous cars could free up billions of collective hours spent driving, allowing users to focus on other activities, many of which could involve Apple's services. In this way, the car was more than a product; it was a platform for Apple to deepen its relationship with consumers, making its ecosystem indispensable in yet another aspect of daily life.

Apple's motivations weren't just about joining the automotive industry; they were about redefining it. The company's vision extended far beyond the car itself, aiming to revolutionize transportation, connectivity, and user experience in ways that only Apple could imagine. This bold ambition, while inspiring, also set a high bar—one that would prove challenging to reach.

The strategic benefits of Apple's venture into autonomous vehicles extended far beyond simply manufacturing a car. At the heart of the idea was the potential to integrate Apple's ecosystem into the driving experience in ways that were both seamless and transformative. Apple had already made strides in the automotive space with CarPlay, its interface for connecting iPhones to car infotainment systems. However, an autonomous Apple car offered the chance to take this integration to an entirely new level.

CarPlay served as a foundation, allowing drivers to access navigation, music, and messages through a familiar Apple-designed interface. But with a fully autonomous vehicle, Apple envisioned a scenario where the car itself became a hub for its ecosystem, untethered from the need for an iPhone or other devices. Passengers would no longer need to focus on driving, freeing them to engage with Apple's apps and services during their journeys. From watching Apple TV+ shows to managing tasks through productivity apps, the possibilities for immersive user experiences were vast.

This concept wasn't just about convenience; it was about creating a new revenue stream. By embedding its ecosystem into the car, Apple could encourage users to spend more time within its digital environment, increasing engagement with its subscription services. The car, in this vision, became not just a mode of transportation but an extension of the Apple experience—one where every moment of travel could be monetized.

Autonomous systems also presented opportunities for new features tied to Apple's strengths. Imagine a car that could automatically sync with a user's Apple Music playlist based on their mood, use advanced machine learning to predict destinations, or even offer voice-controlled commerce, such as ordering food en route. Payment integration for services like EV charging, fuel, and drive-through purchases could all be seamlessly handled through the car's interface, further embedding Apple's ecosystem into daily life.

By tying autonomous cars into its broader ecosystem, Apple wasn't just building a vehicle—it was creating a platform to deepen customer loyalty and generate continuous revenue. This vision of strategic integration underscored the company's bold ambitions, highlighting why it was willing to invest so heavily in Project Titan. The car was a means to expand Apple's presence in users' lives, but the scale of this ambition also brought significant challenges, as the complexity of creating such a vehicle began to unfold.

Chapter 4: Hitting Speed Bumps

From the outset, Apple's ambitious car project faced significant challenges, many of which stemmed from instability at the top. Leadership turbulence became a defining feature of Project Titan, disrupting momentum and creating uncertainty among the thousands of employees involved. Steve Zadesky, the former Ford engineer who had been handpicked to lead the effort, departed the project in 2016 after just a year. While Apple offered no official explanation, reports suggested he left due to personal reasons and mounting frustrations over the lack of clear direction. Zadesky's departure was a blow to the fledgling team, stripping the project of one of its earliest champions.

To stabilize the effort, Apple brought in Bob Mansfield, a respected executive who had previously overseen hardware engineering for some of Apple's most successful products, including the MacBook Air and iPad. Mansfield's return from semi-retirement signaled Apple's determination to salvage the project, but his leadership came with a shift in focus. Instead of pursuing the dream of a fully autonomous vehicle—a goal that seemed increasingly unattainable—Mansfield steered the team toward developing a semi-autonomous car with more conventional capabilities. This pivot reflected a recognition of the immense technological and regulatory hurdles that came with full autonomy, as well as the growing sense that Apple might have overestimated its ability to disrupt the automotive industry.

The decision to scale back ambitions marked a turning point for Project Titan, but it also created internal friction. Many team members who had joined with the promise of working on a revolutionary product found themselves grappling with a watered-down vision. What was once imagined as a driverless car with no steering wheel or pedals was now being reimagined as a more traditional vehicle with advanced driver-assistance features—similar to what Tesla was already offering. For a company like Apple, which prided itself on delivering game-changing innovations, this shift felt like a compromise that undermined the project's original purpose.

The frequent leadership changes and shifting priorities left many employees disillusioned. Reports of confusion and skepticism within the team began to surface, with some employees questioning whether Apple truly had the resolve to see the project through. These internal challenges, combined with the technical difficulties of building a car from scratch, created a perfect storm of obstacles. As the years went on, it became increasingly clear that Project Titan was struggling to find its way, and the dream of revolutionizing transportation was slipping further out of reach.

As Project Titan progressed, internal frustrations began to mount, eroding the morale of the team tasked with bringing Apple's ambitious vision to life. The lack of a clear and consistent direction left many employees unsure of their roles and the ultimate goal of their work. Leadership changes and shifting priorities only added to the confusion, creating an environment where progress felt increasingly difficult to achieve.

For many within the company, the excitement that initially surrounded the project began to give way to skepticism and even cynicism. Reports emerged that some employees outside the Project Titan team openly mocked the effort, referring to it as a vanity project that seemed disconnected from Apple's core strengths. These internal jokes reflected a growing perception that the company was in over its head, venturing into an industry it didn't fully understand.

The sense of disillusionment wasn't limited to outsiders looking in. Within the team itself, employees struggled with the constant changes in strategy and leadership, which often rendered their work obsolete. Engineers and designers would spend months developing features or systems, only to see them discarded as the project's focus shifted yet again. This cycle of rework and uncertainty created a sense of futility among many team members, with some questioning whether the project was destined to succeed at all.

Adding to the frustrations was the pressure to maintain secrecy while competing with established automakers and tech companies. Apple's famously high standards for confidentiality meant that even those within the company often had limited insight into what was happening with the project. This lack of transparency further compounded feelings of isolation and confusion, making it difficult for team members to see how their contributions fit into the bigger picture.

The combination of these factors—unclear leadership, shifting goals, and a lack of cohesion—created an environment where progress was not only slow but also fraught with tension. For a project that began with so much promise, the growing internal frustrations highlighted the challenges of tackling an industry as complex and demanding as automotive manufacturing, even for a company as innovative and resource-rich as Apple. These struggles would ultimately play a significant role in the project's inability to reach its ambitious goals.

Chapter 5: Challenges of Innovation

One of the most significant hurdles Apple faced in its quest to develop a revolutionary vehicle was the sheer complexity of achieving full autonomy. The idea of a car that could navigate streets, highways, and unpredictable environments without human intervention was enticing, but it also represented one of the most challenging technological frontiers of the modern era. Even industry leaders like Tesla, who had been at the forefront of autonomous driving technology for years, were grappling with its limitations.

At the core of the challenge was the need for systems that could process and react to vast amounts of data in real time. Autonomous vehicles require a seamless integration of sensors, cameras, LiDAR, and radar to "see" their surroundings, combined with powerful machine-learning algorithms capable of interpreting and responding to this data with precision. These systems must not only navigate clear conditions but also handle edge cases: unexpected obstacles, unpredictable human behaviors, and diverse weather conditions. For Apple, developing this technology from scratch proved to be a daunting task.

While Apple had deep expertise in software and hardware design, it lacked the years of automotive-specific experience that competitors like Tesla and Waymo had accrued. Companies already entrenched in the autonomous vehicle space had spent decades refining their technologies and building the infrastructure needed for testing and deployment. Apple, by contrast, was starting from the ground up, trying to leapfrog the competition with a revolutionary product. This lack of foundational experience became a significant disadvantage.

Compounding the difficulty was the fact that full autonomy requires more than technological breakthroughs—it also demands navigating complex regulatory landscapes. Governments around the world have been cautious in approving fully autonomous systems for public roads, requiring exhaustive testing and validation to ensure safety. Apple's lack of a publicly available product meant it was trailing behind companies like Tesla, which already had semi-autonomous features on the market and were gathering real-world data to improve their systems.

Despite its vast resources and ambition, Apple found itself confronting the reality that full autonomy was a goal far more challenging than it had initially anticipated. Even with billions invested, the company struggled to close the gap between its vision and what was technologically and practically feasible. This inability to overcome the barriers of autonomy was a critical factor in the eventual scaling back of Project Titan, highlighting the immense difficulty of innovating in an industry where the stakes—and the challenges—are extraordinarily high.

As Apple navigated the complex and highly competitive landscape of autonomous vehicle development, it encountered significant legal and ethical challenges that further complicated Project Titan. Among the most high-profile issues were incidents involving employee misconduct and trade secret theft. Several employees were accused of stealing confidential information related to the project, with allegations that some had shared these secrets with competing companies or foreign entities. In one particularly troubling case, a former Apple engineer was arrested while attempting to board a flight to China, allegedly carrying sensitive Project Titan documents.

These incidents not only exposed vulnerabilities in Apple's famously secretive operations but also underscored the high stakes of autonomous vehicle development. The automotive and tech industries were locked in an arms race for talent and intellectual property, with companies vying to gain an edge in a field that promised to reshape transportation. For Apple, these legal entanglements distracted from the already immense technical and logistical challenges of the project, while raising questions about the company's ability to safeguard its innovations.

Safety concerns during testing added another layer of complexity. Autonomous vehicles must undergo rigorous evaluation to ensure their reliability in real-world scenarios, and Apple's test cars were no exception. However, an incident in 2022 involving a near-collision between an Apple test vehicle and a jogger highlighted the risks associated with the technology. Although no harm was done, the close call underscored the critical importance of safety in autonomous driving—a standard that even small missteps could jeopardize.

Beyond these internal and operational challenges, Apple faced fierce competition in the broader market. Tesla, the undisputed leader in electric vehicles, had set a high bar with its lineup of semi-autonomous cars and established a loyal customer base. The company's Autopilot system, while not perfect, was years ahead of

Apple's efforts, benefiting from extensive real-world testing and continuous updates. Tesla's dominance in both market share and public perception made it a formidable rival.

At the same time, emerging startups like Rivian were carving out niches in the EV market, offering innovative designs and technologies that appealed to a new generation of consumers. Rivian's focus on adventure-ready vehicles and partnerships with major players like Amazon gave it a strong foothold, further crowding the space Apple hoped to enter. Established automakers such as General Motors and Ford were also investing heavily in their own EV and autonomous driving initiatives, leveraging decades of industry experience to stay competitive.

For Apple, the combination of internal setbacks, legal and ethical challenges, and intense market competition created a perfect storm of obstacles. Even with its reputation for innovation and vast financial resources, the company found itself struggling to stand out in an industry where the stakes were higher, and the margins for error were smaller, than it had ever encountered before. These pressures would ultimately contribute to the scaling back—and eventual cancellation—of its ambitious car project.

Chapter 6: Apple's Expensive Gamble

Over the course of a decade, Apple poured an estimated $10 billion into Project Titan, making it one of the most expensive ventures in the company's history. For a business that consistently turned record-breaking profits, the investment might not have seemed overly risky at first. However, as the years passed and tangible results remained elusive, the staggering cost of the project began to raise eyebrows, both internally and among industry observers.

The scale of Apple's financial commitment reflected its determination to compete in the rapidly evolving automotive market. The company allocated substantial resources to research and development, hiring thousands of engineers, designers, and automotive experts.

Beyond personnel costs, Apple also invested heavily in state-of-the-art facilities, cutting-edge technology, and partnerships aimed at accelerating progress.

A significant portion of this spending went toward scaling up testing efforts in California, where Apple deployed a fleet of autonomous test vehicles on public roads. These cars, equipped with advanced sensor arrays and proprietary software, were registered with the state's Department of Motor Vehicles under the guise of corporate anonymity. At one point, Apple had more test vehicles registered in California than both Uber and Waymo, signaling the seriousness of its ambitions.

To bolster its capabilities, Apple also turned to acquisitions. In 2019, the company purchased Drive.ai, a startup specializing in artificial intelligence for autonomous vehicles. The acquisition not only brought valuable technology into Apple's fold but also added a team of talented engineers and researchers with deep expertise in self-driving systems. Drive.ai was just one example of Apple's strategy to acquire smaller firms that could fill gaps in its own knowledge and infrastructure, a pattern the company had successfully employed in other industries.

Despite these massive investments, progress remained slow. The complexity of autonomous driving technology, combined with leadership instability and shifting priorities, meant that much of the money spent failed to yield the transformative breakthroughs Apple had hoped for. Testing efforts, while extensive, were marred by incidents and setbacks that highlighted the challenges of achieving full autonomy.

Acquisitions like Drive.ai added valuable resources, but they were not enough to bridge the widening gap between Apple's ambitions and its results.

As the years went on, the $10 billion price tag loomed larger. For a company known for its precise execution and unparalleled profitability, the lack of a clear return on investment stood out as an anomaly. While Apple could absorb the financial hit, the growing perception of Project Titan as a money pit contributed to mounting pressure to reconsider its viability. In the end, the extraordinary expense, coupled with a lack of tangible progress, became one of the key factors in the project's ultimate demise.

Despite Apple's vast resources, talent pool, and reputation for innovation, the company ultimately could not deliver on its ambitious vision for the Apple car. The failure to bring Project Titan to fruition was not due to a single issue but rather a convergence of challenges that proved insurmountable, even for one of the world's most successful tech giants.

One of the most significant barriers was the sheer complexity of the undertaking. Unlike consumer electronics, where Apple had decades of expertise, building a car—especially a fully autonomous one—required mastering an entirely different set of skills and technologies. The automotive industry operates on long product cycles, intricate supply chains, and rigorous safety standards, all of which were new territory for Apple. While the company excelled in software and design, it lacked the foundational knowledge and infrastructure of established automakers, forcing it to rely heavily on partnerships and acquisitions, which often proved insufficient.

Leadership instability further exacerbated these challenges. The constant turnover at the top of Project Titan created confusion and disrupted momentum. Each new leader brought a different vision and strategy, leading to frequent shifts in priorities and wasted effort. Engineers would dedicate months to developing systems or features, only to see them abandoned or reimagined with every new change in direction. This lack of continuity undermined the team's ability to make consistent progress.

Compounding these issues were the technical and regulatory hurdles of developing a fully autonomous vehicle. Self-driving technology remains one of the most difficult engineering problems of our time, even for companies like

Tesla and Waymo, which have been working on it for years. Apple, starting from scratch, found itself struggling to match the pace of its competitors. The safety standards required for such technology were unforgiving, and the slightest misstep could tarnish Apple's reputation for quality and reliability.

Market competition also played a critical role in Apple's inability to deliver. Tesla, with its early dominance in the electric vehicle market, had already set high expectations for what a cutting-edge car should be. Startups like Rivian and legacy automakers like General Motors and Volkswagen were also innovating rapidly, leaving little room for Apple to differentiate itself. In this crowded and fast-evolving space, Apple faced the daunting challenge of catching up while simultaneously trying to leap ahead—a near-impossible balancing act.

Finally, the sheer scale of the investment and the lack of visible progress created mounting pressure both internally and externally. Apple had spent nearly $10 billion on a project that had yet to produce a marketable product. The company's leadership faced tough questions about whether continuing to invest in Project Titan made sense, especially as other priorities, like artificial intelligence, began to emerge.

In the end, Apple's failure to deliver on its ambitious car project was a reminder that even the most resource-rich companies are not immune to the complexities and challenges of entering unfamiliar industries. The dream of revolutionizing transportation, while inspiring, proved to be an endeavor fraught with obstacles that even Apple could not overcome. This failure stands as a case study in the limits of ambition, showing that success requires not just vision and resources but also focus, expertise, and a realistic understanding of what can be achieved.

Chapter 7: The Decision to Pull the Plug

In February 2024, after nearly a decade of effort, Apple officially pulled the plug on Project Titan, marking the end of its ambitious attempt to create an autonomous vehicle. The announcement came quietly through an internal memo, confirming what many had long suspected: Apple's foray into the automotive industry had reached a dead end. The decision was both surprising and inevitable, reflecting the mounting challenges and diminishing returns the project had faced over the years.

The cancellation wasn't framed as a complete loss but rather as a strategic redirection. Key staff members from Project Titan were reassigned to Apple's artificial intelligence division, a move that signaled the company's pivot toward AI as its next major focus. In the memo, Apple emphasized that the expertise gained during the car project—particularly in machine learning, robotics, and hardware integration—would be instrumental in advancing its broader AI ambitions. This repurposing of talent allowed Apple to salvage some value from the effort, even as it closed the book on its automotive aspirations.

The reasons for the cancellation were multifaceted. Leadership instability, technical and regulatory hurdles, and fierce market competition had all contributed to the project's struggles. By 2024, it had become clear that achieving full autonomy remained a distant goal, one that even the most advanced companies in the field were still grappling with. Apple's original vision of a driverless car with no steering wheel or pedals had long since been scaled back, and even the more modest goal of a semi-autonomous vehicle seemed increasingly out of reach.

Financial pressures also played a role. With nearly $10 billion spent and no viable product to show for it, continuing the project had become difficult to justify. Investors and analysts were beginning to question whether Apple's resources could be better allocated elsewhere, particularly as the company faced new opportunities in artificial intelligence. The AI landscape had exploded in the wake of breakthroughs from companies like OpenAI, and Apple appeared determined not to miss its chance to lead in this transformative area.

The cancellation of Project Titan marked a sobering moment for Apple, a company that had built its reputation on taking bold risks and succeeding against the odds. Yet it also demonstrated the company's pragmatism. Rather than continuing to pour resources into a project with no clear path to success, Apple chose to cut its losses and redirect its focus to areas where it could make a more immediate impact.

While Project Titan may not have achieved its lofty goals, its legacy endures in the lessons it taught Apple about ambition, innovation, and the challenges of entering new industries. The expertise and technologies developed during the car project have not gone to waste but are instead fueling Apple's push into AI, a field that promises to reshape the future in ways as profound as the autonomous car once seemed to. This pivot underscores Apple's ability to adapt and reimagine its role in a rapidly changing technological landscape, even in the face of failure.

The failure of Apple's Project Titan stemmed from a combination of leadership challenges, technical difficulties, and shifting market priorities—factors that, together, created a perfect storm of obstacles. At its core, the project struggled to maintain a consistent vision, a problem that was exacerbated by frequent changes in leadership. Over the course of nearly a decade, the project saw multiple leadership transitions, each accompanied by a redefinition of goals. Steve Zadesky, the project's original leader, departed early, and subsequent leaders, including Bob Mansfield, brought their own approaches, leading to conflicting strategies and repeated setbacks. This instability made it difficult for the team to achieve cohesion, and much of the work undertaken was abandoned or reworked as priorities shifted.

On the technical side, Apple faced a challenge more formidable than it had likely anticipated. The development of a fully autonomous vehicle required solving problems that even the most advanced companies in the field, like Tesla and Waymo, had yet to fully conquer. The complexity of creating reliable autonomous systems capable of navigating unpredictable real-world environments proved to be a daunting task. Apple, despite its expertise in software and hardware integration, lacked the automotive-specific knowledge and infrastructure to compete on equal footing with companies that had been working in the space for years. Safety incidents during testing further highlighted the steep learning curve Apple faced.

Market dynamics also played a critical role in the project's failure. When Apple first began exploring the idea of an autonomous vehicle, the field was relatively new, and the potential for disruption seemed immense. However, as years passed, competition intensified. Tesla solidified its dominance in the electric vehicle market, while startups like Rivian and legacy automakers like General Motors and Volkswagen made significant strides in their own autonomous and electric vehicle efforts. By the time Apple was ready to scale back its ambitions to focus on a semi-autonomous car, the market had become far more crowded, leaving little room for Apple to differentiate itself.

The lessons from Project Titan's failure are stark but invaluable. Overambition was a key misstep. Apple entered the automotive industry with the goal of revolutionizing it, aiming for a level of innovation that was not just challenging but, given the state of technology, likely unattainable within the timeline it envisioned. This overreach diverted significant resources into a project that lacked the clear focus needed to succeed in such a competitive and complex field. Instead of starting with incremental goals and building expertise, Apple aimed directly for the top, leaving itself vulnerable to the pitfalls of inexperience and overconfidence.

Another critical lesson was the importance of focus and alignment. Apple's greatest successes—products like the iPhone, iPod, and Mac—were born from a clear and cohesive vision, executed with precision. In contrast, Project Titan suffered from a lack of direction, with shifting objectives and unclear leadership eroding the team's ability to make steady progress. This fragmentation highlighted the risks of venturing too far from a company's core strengths without a solid foundation and roadmap.

While the failure of Project Titan was undoubtedly a setback, it also served as a reminder of the challenges that come with pushing the boundaries of innovation. For Apple, these lessons will likely inform its approach to future projects, ensuring that the company remains focused on what it does best: creating transformative products with clarity, purpose, and unparalleled attention to detail.

Chapter 8: What Comes Next?

After the cancellation of Project Titan in 2024, Apple swiftly pivoted its focus to artificial intelligence, a field that had been gaining momentum globally and presented vast opportunities for innovation. The expertise and technologies developed during the car project—particularly in areas like machine learning, robotics, and data processing—were not abandoned but repurposed to strengthen Apple's AI initiatives. Employees from Project Titan were reassigned to roles supporting AI-driven projects, signaling a clear shift in priorities. This move aligned with Apple's broader strategy of integrating AI into its existing ecosystem, enhancing products like Siri, iPhone, and Mac with more advanced capabilities.

Apple's pivot to AI was not merely a reactive decision but a calculated one, reflecting its recognition of the transformative potential of artificial intelligence. The company began acquiring a slew of AI startups, bolstering its talent pool and technology base. It also intensified efforts to develop proprietary AI tools, aiming to redefine user experiences across its devices and services. This shift demonstrated Apple's adaptability, leveraging the lessons learned from Project Titan to gain a foothold in a domain that promised to reshape industries globally.

Even as Apple exited the car manufacturing race, it remained a significant player in the automotive world through its CarPlay platform. CarPlay, which allows iPhone users to connect seamlessly with their vehicle's infotainment system, had become a standard feature in 98% of new cars sold in the United States by 2024. This dominance represented a quiet but effective "Trojan horse" strategy, embedding Apple's ecosystem deeply into the automotive experience without the need to produce a car itself.

CarPlay's success lay in its simplicity and integration. It offered drivers access to navigation, music, calls, and messages through an intuitive interface, making Apple devices indispensable in daily commutes. Moreover, CarPlay positioned Apple as a key intermediary between automakers and consumers, granting it valuable insights into user behavior and preferences while expanding the reach of its services. This strategy allowed Apple to maintain influence in the automotive space without taking on the immense risks and complexities of manufacturing vehicles.

Looking ahead, the question remains: could Apple revisit the automotive industry with a different approach? While the failure of Project Titan demonstrated the challenges of entering the car market, it also provided Apple with invaluable experience and a deeper understanding of the industry. Some speculate that Apple could focus on developing advanced software and autonomous driving systems rather than manufacturing entire vehicles. By partnering with established automakers, Apple could leverage its strengths in design and technology while avoiding the pitfalls of building and selling cars.

Another possibility is that Apple could return to the car market when the technology and regulatory landscape for autonomy matures. The company has a history of entering markets late but dominating them through superior execution, as seen with the iPhone. If Apple were to revisit the idea of a car, it would likely do so with a more focused strategy, targeting specific areas where it can innovate and add value.

For now, Apple's pivot to AI and the dominance of CarPlay underscore its ability to adapt and thrive in a rapidly changing technological landscape. Whether or not it decides to take the wheel again, Apple's influence in the automotive industry remains strong, and its legacy of ambition and innovation continues to shape its path forward.

Conclusion

The story of Apple's ambitious yet ultimately unsuccessful car project stands as a powerful testament to the complexities of innovation and the inherent risks of venturing beyond one's core expertise. Project Titan was a bold attempt to redefine the automotive industry, driven by the same spirit of ambition and ingenuity that had propelled Apple to global dominance in consumer electronics. Yet, the challenges it faced—technical, organizational, and strategic—revealed the limits of even the most resource-rich companies when tackling entirely new industries.

At its heart, the Apple car story underscores the delicate balance between ambition and focus. Innovation thrives on big ideas, but without a clear and cohesive strategy, even the most visionary projects can falter. Apple's struggles with leadership instability, shifting goals, and the immense technical hurdles of full autonomy serve as a cautionary tale about the importance of alignment and expertise. While Apple's strengths in software and design were undeniable, the complexities of automotive manufacturing and the pace of competition proved to be formidable obstacles.

The broader implications of this case extend far beyond Apple. For companies across industries, it highlights the importance of understanding one's core competencies and the risks of overextending into unfamiliar territory. At the same time, it demonstrates the value of learning from failure. Apple's pivot to artificial intelligence and its continued dominance in the automotive ecosystem through CarPlay show how companies can adapt, leveraging setbacks as opportunities for growth and redirection.

Despite its ultimate cancellation, the Apple car project left a lasting impact on the automotive space. It fueled speculation, inspired innovation, and raised the bar for what a technology company could aspire to achieve. The lessons from Project Titan continue to influence Apple's approach to new ventures, ensuring that the company remains a formidable force in the ever-evolving world of technology.

Apple's attempt to revolutionize transportation may have fallen short, but its boldness in taking on such an audacious challenge reflects the same drive that has defined its greatest successes. Even in failure, Apple's willingness to push boundaries and explore uncharted territories leaves an indelible mark, reminding us that the pursuit of innovation is as much about resilience and adaptation as it is about achieving the extraordinary.

www.ingramcontent.com/pod-product-compliance
Lightning Source LLC
Chambersburg PA
CBHW070412230526
45471CB00006B/2763